POCKET STUDY SKILLS

Series Editor: **Kate Williams**,
Oxford Brookes University, UK
Illustrations by Sallie Godwin

For the time-pushed student, the *Pocket Study Skills* pack a lot of advice into a little book. Each guide focuses on a single crucial aspect of study, giving you step-by-step guidance, handy tips and clear advice on how to approach the important areas which will continually be at the core of your studies.

Pocket Study Skills
Series Standing Order
ISBN 978-0-230-21605-1
(outside North America only)

You can receive future titles in this series as they are published by placing a standing order. Please contact your bookseller or, in case of difficulty, write to us at the address below with your name and address, the title of the series and the ISBN quoted above.

Customer Services Department, Macmillan Distribution Ltd, Houndmills, Basingstoke, Hampshire, RG21 6XS, UK

Published

14 Days to Exam Success
Blogs, Wikis, Podcasts and More
Brilliant Writing Tips for Students
Completing Your PhD
Doing Research
Getting Critical (2nd edn)
Planning Your Dissertation
Planning Your Essay (2nd edn)
Planning Your PhD
Posters and Presentations
Reading and Making Notes (2nd edn)
Referencing and Understanding Plagiarism
Reflective Writing
Report Writing
Science Study Skills
Studying with Dyslexia
Success in Groupwork
Time Management
Writing for University

POCKET STUDY SKILLS

Kate Williams

GETTING CRITICAL

SECOND EDITION

First edition 2009
Second edition 2014

First published 2009 by
PALGRAVE MACMILLAN

Palgrave Macmillan in the UK is an imprint of Macmillan Publishers Limited, registered in England, company number 785998, of 4 Crinan Street, London N1 9XW.

Palgrave Macmillan in the US is a division of St Martin's Press LLC, 175 Fifth Avenue, New York, NY 10010.

Palgrave Macmillan is the global academic imprint of the above companies and has companies and representatives throughout the world.

Palgrave® and Macmillan® are registered trademarks in the United States, the United Kingdom, Europe and other countries

ISBN: 978-1-137-40251-6

This book is printed on paper suitable for recycling and made from fully managed and sustained forest sources. Logging, pulping and manufacturing processes are expected to conform to the environmental regulations of the country of origin.

A catalogue record for this book is available from the British Library.

Contents

Acknowledgements

Many people have contributed to this guide – both to the original book and to this updated second edition – and I would like to thank them all. First, of course, my thanks to the students who have discussed their dilemmas and shared their 'Eureka!' moments, allowing me to bring the outcomes of these private conversations to a wider audience.

I am hugely grateful to critical readers of the first edition, who have shown me their favourite pages, and allowed me the benefits of hindsight: you will see I have added some material and clarified other points in this new edition.

Special thanks to students who gave their permission to use extracts from their work: Aline, Tom, Yiannis and Adrienne; and to colleagues at Oxford Brookes University for their advice: Hazel Rothera on online searching; to Mary Woolliams, Dan Butcher and Jim Pye on critical thinking in healthcare; Berry O'Donovan on assessment criteria in the Business School.

The author and publishers wish to thank the following for permission to reproduce copyright material: Open University for 'critical thinking' from their website; Elsevier for permission for the article by Osborne and Kiker.

Finally, thanks to Sallie Godwin for her illustrations, as astute as ever, and to Suzannah Burywood and colleagues at Palgrave Macmillan for their support and endless patience and creativity.

Introduction

> *Your account is too descriptive ...*

> *You need to show more analysis in your work ...*

> *You need to question the findings in more detail ...*

> *You need to be more critical ...*

If you have ever had feedback like this on your work and wondered what it means, why it matters and what you should do about it, then this guide is for you.

The guide has been written to show students:

- what being 'critical' means in higher education
- how to bring that 'critical' dimension into all aspects of your work.

Being 'critical' at university

The word 'critical' has several meanings in everyday life, most commonly:

- finding fault: a negative comment such as *not good enough*; *sloppily done*; *could do better*; *why didn't you …?*
- key, decisive, crucial: as in *'a critical moment'*, *'critically ill'*, *'a critical decision'*.

Neither of these is the meaning of 'critical' when describing the quality tutors want to see in students' work. 'Critical' in university work means being thoughtful, asking questions, not taking things you read (or hear) at face value. It means finding information and understanding different approaches and using them in your writing.

A critical approach is not a form of writing in itself (like an essay or report), nor a particular 'hat' you put on from time to time when you read, or an optional add-on. It is a mindset you need for life and work, and very much part of the wider picture of having a methodical and thoughtful approach to your studies. When you find your own questioning 'critical' approach (and you will!), you and your studies will take off.

Being 'critical': why does it matter?

Consider these mini scenarios: why does being 'critical' matter in each?

Scenario 1

You like the wind in your hair. Is it really worth wearing a cycle helmet? Of course you know the advice is to wear one, but you need convincing. What evidence underpins this recommendation? Is it the outcome of systematic research by people who have:

- treated head injuries
- studied accident statistics
- done this in several settings, by methods set out clearly
- and reached the conclusions which led to this recommendation?

And do you change your behaviour? That's your choice!

The 'critical' bit? When specialists – or you – study the studies, they need to 'think critically' about the quality of the evidence, and the way the studies were carried out. The conclusions are only as good as the methods.

The 'critical' bit? You read the book thoughtfully to understand Conrad's attitudes. You ask questions about when and how the concept of 'racism' developed, relate it to him and his time, and reach a conclusion. The question matters because concepts shape societies and individuals' experiences within them.

Scenario 3

You think your child is finding it hard to learn to read. What do you want from the teacher? Probably someone who:

▸ knows what to expect in most children
▸ reflects on your child in relation to the milestones
▸ chooses an approach to use with your child from the range she knows about
▸ will review and try another approach ... and so on ...

The 'critical' bit? This practitioner – the teacher – has knowledge and understanding, and is able to apply it. She reflects and thinks about the individual child to evaluate what is going well and not so well, and to develop her approach accordingly.

Scenario 4

Your decision to study at your chosen institution will have been the outcome of hard critical thinking, balancing up different factors:

▸ subject, and combination of topics
▸ university – entry requirements, particular characteristics or opportunities
▸ location – country, city, proximity to ...?

And other factors, such as cost of housing, job/career opportunities ...

The 'critical' bit? You don't rely on one source of information: you balance the university's glossy prospectus against official data. You look closely at university league tables to try and see what they are measuring and how. You talk to friends at uni (whose judgement do you trust?). You visit.

You think critically: you evaluate the reliability of sources of evidence; you pick your way through conflicting accounts and priorities. Ultimately, you match all this with you and what you want, and make this critical decision.

All these situations show a 'critical' awareness. This dimension informs policies, decisions and actions; attitudes and awareness; professional good practice – and more. It is an essential quality to bring to life and work.

So what's new at university?

Not a lot. You are naturally critical most of the time. You know that (some) newspaper reports only give half the story; that 'buy one, get one free' in one supermarket is still more expensive than the straight price in another; that you'd go and see a film one friend recommends, and steer clear of someone else's recommendations. You discriminate, make judgements, set one view against another, and ultimately take responsibility for your own judgements and actions.

All you've got to do is to carry this over into your studies. You are not a sponge, soaking up knowledge, and squeezing it out in your assignments to prove you 'know' it. You entered university as a thoughtful and questioning person, and your course is an opportunity for you to develop these qualities in a new context.

About this guide

This book is about how you *do* this:

Part 1: Getting a critical mindset is about taking a strategic approach to your studies right from the start: understanding the language of the guidance you are given and how you are assessed.

Part 2: Getting critical in research and reading is about bringing this critical mindset to all aspects of your research and reading, from reading lists to notes and record keeping.

Part 3: Getting critical in writing takes a methodical look at the key processes in writing an essay or assignment, and what your (critical) reader will expect.

Part 4: Critical steps takes a closer look at using a 'framework' for critical analysis and revisits the language used to describe these critical skills.

Kate Williams

GETTING A CRITICAL MINDSET

1 Getting strategic

Part 1 takes a good look at how to get that critical mindset in your studies. It's all about asking questions – right from the beginning, before you dive into your courses.

- Chapter 1 sets out six strategic questions that you can use again and again throughout your studies to get a fix on any task or assignment you are set.
- Chapter 2 invites you to take a close look at what your lecturers are looking for when they assess your work, and what assessment criteria mean in practice.
- Chapter 3 defines many of the terms you will encounter in relation to critical thinking.

As you go through the book, you will gain more insight into what these qualities look like in practice, and how you can develop them in your own work.

Six **strategic questions** are used by many people to get themselves started in tackling a task, whether it's planning a project, getting to grips with reading, or writing something:

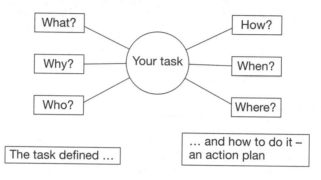

Try this in relation to your course handbook, or materials for one module or unit.

A strategic reading of a course handbook!

You may not have one single handbook for each course or module you are taking, setting out the programme and assessment tasks for the term or semester. If your materials are online (on Moodle, for example) you may have to compile your own 'course handbook' from several documents. Get hunting!

These documents contain essential guidance. Somewhere in there it will tell you what you have to do, and often quite a lot about how to set about it, as well as the practicalities – like when it needs to be done by.

Your critical approach to your studies starts here! Check through these materials and read them carefully to make sure you have all the information you need to answer the strategic questions.

The task defined

The first three key questions (on the left in the table) will help you to get the measure of the task(s) you have been set.

What exactly do you have to produce?	… in your next essay/ assignment?
What format? Essay? Report? Specific format? Presentation? Tests?	
Any guidance about structure, layout and style?	
How long?	
What % marks does the task count for?	
What topic(s)?	

Why are you being asked to do this?	
External reasons: the 'learning outcomes' you are expected to achieve.	
Internal reasons: your private purpose – interest in the subject, personal satisfaction.	

Who are you writing for? It helps you write if you can visualise your reader.	
Your tutor is always your audience. What do you know about what s/he wants to see?	
Do you have another real audience, for example giving a presentation to your seminar group?	
Or an imagined audience, like writing a report (for a company for example), or an article for a particular journal?	

Most writing tasks do not specify an audience (beyond the obvious – your tutor or a colleague). You may find it helpful to imagine a 'default' audience when you write.

> **Write as if …**
>
> … you are addressing someone with the same experience and knowledge of the general subject area as yourself, but who has not yet covered this particular topic/module/course. If you do this you will not be tempted to:
>
> ▶ talk up, using fancy language designed to impress
> ▶ talk down, with an inappropriate informal or chatty style.
>
> Talk on their level, using clear, simple language; use short sentences; and draw on the specialist language, conventions and style of your subject when you need to.

And how to do it – an action plan

How ...? What guidance are you given about what to include?	... in your next essay/ assignment?
For example: Use of appendices? Style of referencing? Acceptable and unacceptable practice?	

When ...? is the deadline for the final hand-in?	
Are there earlier deadlines for drafts and various elements?	
How will you balance working towards one deadline with working towards others? And life, job etc.?	

Where ...? will you find the information?	
How much of it is easy to find (course readers, textbooks, special collections)?	
How much do you have to research yourself? And go beyond the reading list?	

Your answers to these questions will help you work out an action plan for getting it done. You may like to try some of these suggestions:

- Complete a term or semester timeline.
- List the specifics: break down major tasks from the timeline into small tasks.
- Check your diary – for job schedules, weekends away, a social life even …
- Plan your week: look for short start-up slots, longer working chunks, short review slots.
- Write 'to do' lists (make each item a small one!), and tick them off when you have done them.

For more suggestions, see *Time Management* in this series.

Now take a closer look at the specific guidance you have been given about what tutors are looking for in what you write, and how it will be assessed. This is where you get to grips with the language of assessment – which at first glance can appear rather a **critical soup** …

These phrases come from the assessment criteria for a top grade from a range of subject areas in a number of universities. You will notice that *critical analysis*, *evaluation*, *thinking* are words consistently linked with higher grades:

> *Good example of critical thinking in looking at the issue from more than one perspective.* (B+)

And the lack of that critical dimension often explains a lower grade:

> *What are the implications of this word? Try to be more critical in your reading.* (C)

Assessment criteria: what are they looking for?

Tutors are often better at placing a piece of work in a particular grade than at articulating why they did it. Assessment criteria are an attempt both to express the intellectual qualities tutors are looking for, and to explain their subsequent grading.

Assessment criteria take many forms: some describe the qualities of each grade in a paragraph; others set them out as a grid (as below). Some are specific to each assignment or essay; others are generic – used across a course, department, Faculty or School. Whatever they look like, you need to look at them and quiz them before you start.

Example 1: Qualities + grading

In this style of sheet the qualities (or 'criteria') are listed on the left, and grades, set out in various ways, head the columns. It gives you a checklist of what the marker will be looking for.

Try turning assessment criteria into a checklist for yourself by answering the questions about what each phrase means.

Criteria/qualities	A	B+	B	C	F
Knowledge and understanding Level of subject knowledge Able to identify key debates Understands relevant concepts and theory					
Evidence and analysis Logical development of argument Evaluation of source material Evidence provided to support case					
Reading and research Selection of appropriate material Effective use of a wide range of material Evidence of independent research					
Presentation Clarity of expression Clear and accurate referencing					

In your next assignment ...

What are the key debates?

What concepts and theories should you know about? Which are relevant to this question?

In one sentence, what are you going to say? What points do you want to make?

How do the various things you have read support the points you want to make? Or not?

What does 'wide range' mean? How many sources? What sort?

... going beyond the reading list

How will you tackle the reading? And pick and choose what you use and what you don't?

Example 2: Qualities defined

This style of feedback sheet is longer (often several pages), and aims to define more precisely what the grade means in relation to each quality or criterion. You need a focus when you look at these pages: study the top grade criteria to see what the marker Is looking for.

In these extracts, only 'Intellectual skills' is shown.

	Knowledge and understanding	Reading and research	**Intellectual skills**	Presentation
70+ A			Develops coherent, logical and relevant arguments, drawing appropriate conclusions. Demonstrates depth of critical analysis and independent thought.	

Argument again – clearly a top of the tree quality. You can only work out an argument when you have done the foundations - read, understood - and worked with it - thought and planned.

Must have a good conclusion. Note the 's'. Several strands drawn together.

Really understanding what the articles say, how they support each other, how they differ – and showing you see this ... Hm...

Your own perspective ... and evidence for it ....

Look at the lower grades to see what you need to go beyond.

60–69 B+			Well-developed argument. Demonstrates independent thought and critical analysis.	
50–59 B			Develops some arguments. Demonstrates critical thinking in a straightforward manner.	
40–49 C			Assembles and links ideas.	
Fail, resit etc.			Development of argument is weak and/or a purely descriptive account throughout. Conclusions inappropriate or absent. Unsubstantiated claims based on anecdotes/generalisations.	

Setting out brief summaries of what you have read, even when you relate them to each other, will get you a basic pass.

Simply setting down what you have read, done or heard without comment is not enough..

Conclusions must flow from the rest of the writing.

You need evidence which itself is well founded for the statements you make.

The description of the qualities expected in students' work will of course vary from subject to subject, tutor to tutor, one university to another. There will, however, be a consistent core of shared values and definitions of what markers expect to see.

3 The stairway to critical thinking

There is no shortage of definitions and attempts to describe the qualities associated with critical thinking.[1] A definition is a good place to start when you are trying to understand something, and useful here to see what assessment criteria are based on.

The diagram on p. 14 sets out the 'stairway' to critical thinking as described by the Open University (2008). In it you will recognise some of the terms used in assessment criteria and throughout this guide.

Start at the bottom. The first four steps suggest approaches to getting to grips with your reading and research. Your writing task may ask you to record this: *describe, analyse, compare*. The top four steps show some of the key functions you are asked to do in your writing. Some of these may appear in your essay title: *evaluate, apply, justify*. These terms are considered in more detail in Chapter 14 (Part 4).

Tick all the processes you think you will have to do for your next assignment, and highlight the words and phrases that appear in the assessment criteria.

---

1 See 'Useful sources' for additional sources and brief comments.

The stairway to critical thinking

							Justify
Use critical thinking to develop arguments, draw conclusions, make inferences and identify implications.							
Transfer the understanding you have gained from your critical evaluation and use in response to questions, assignments and projects.						Apply	
Assess the worth of an idea in terms of its relevance to your needs, the evidence on which it is based and how it relates to other pertinent ideas.					Evaluate		
Bring together different sources to serve an argument or idea you are constructing. Make logical connections between the different sources that help you shape and support your ideas.				Synthesise			
			Compare	Explore the similarities and differences between the ideas you are reading about.			
		Analyse	Examine how these key components fit together and relate to each other.				
Start here ☺	Understand	Comprehend the key points, assumptions, arguments and evidence presented.					
Process	Take in the information, i.e. what you have read, heard, seen or done.						

Source: 'Critical Thinking', © 2013 The Open University. Used with permission. The OU text has been drawn as a stairway.

Definitions are not enough!

Of course, definitions alone are not enough to offer useful guidance about what you need to *do* to get that critical dimension into your work. Examples, models, outlines, conversation and discussion (and this book of course!) all help to translate the abstract definition into a practical understanding of what you need to put on the page.

And note …

Not every piece of work requires you to be operating on the top steps for a top grade. Sometimes you will be asked to 'describe', 'trace', 'explain', and it will be possible to get a top grade for it because the process is exceptionally complex, difficult, hard to disentangle. Here it is key for you to demonstrate your understanding. In essays and assignments, however, there is a correlation between the top, middle and lower steps, and the top, middle and lower grades. (See *Planning Your Essay* in this series.)

So, how do I get critical?

That critical quality will grow out of a methodical and thoughtful approach to your work – rather like the diagram on the next page. Chapter numbers are shown in brackets.

- Talk to your reader.
- Make it easy for them to follow from start to finish.
- Let your voice shine through.

Start here

Understand what you need to

- do (1)
- know about what your tutors are looking for (2)
- understand about how to achieve this (3)

Growing ideas: Getting critical in writing

- Getting critical with the question (and planning your answer) (10)
- A critical skill – writing paragraphs (11)
- Critical writing and argument (12)

Foundations: Getting critical in research and reading

- Choosing your reading: core, further, and off-list items (4)
- Finding those off-list items: articles, reports, web sources (5)
- And assessing whether they are any good – or not! (6)
- Being selective in what you read, using abstracts (7)
- Becoming strategic in your reading (8)
- And keeping a critical record of what you read (9)

GETTING CRITICAL IN RESEARCH AND READING

I can't read all that!

A critical approach to reading starts before you have read anything …

Critical reading starts with thinking – about what you know already, and what you need to find out. This in turn is driven by the task you have been set (or have set yourself), or the essay question you have to answer.

Take a look at the essay 'questions' in Part 3 (pp. 54–60). You can see here how to pick the question apart, ask questions about it, and identify the topic areas you will need to research.

Try this with your task or question:

This analysis will give you a focus for your research and reading. Now you are ready to start.

Part 2 tracks this process of critical research and reading. By the end, when you come back to your question, you will be ready to plan and write it.

Before you can start your research, make sure you have the baseline introduction to your subject – the two or three items often highlighted as 'essential' or listed week by week. You need these to make sense of the lectures and seminars: it's the place to start.

Reading lists can be daunting. If the list you are looking at is longer than one side, you can be sure you are not expected to read everything on it for one assignment or standard essay. Think of it as suggestions from which you compile your own reading list. Your list will consist of:

- core materials you really do need to read from week to week to keep on top of your course and contribute to discussions
- further reading which will enable you understand some of the complexities; and
- some off-list items you have found yourself as you pursue an interest.

This mix will ensure you are getting the 'wide range' of source material that underpins the higher grades.

Textbooks are helpful in mapping the territory outlining the knowledge areas you need. They may also point out or describe areas of debate and discussion. For the debate itself, or specific studies that draw specific conclusions or develop an argument, you need to read journal articles.

So you need to have an idea about what each item is likely to offer as a basis for selecting what to read. You can tell a lot about a source just by thinking about the information in the reference.

Below (on the left) are extracts from the reading lists of specific modules, and (on the right) what you can tell about each source before you put it on your list.

Healthcare module:

On the reading list	What to expect?
Montague SE, Watson R and Herbert RA (2005). *Physiology for Nurses*, 3rd edition. London: Elsevier.	A general nursing textbook. Good for core knowledge. Check to see if there is a more recent edition.
Devendra D, Lui E and Eisenbarth G (2004). Type I diabetes: recent developments. *British Medical Journal*. l3:28, 750–54.	A journal article (four pages). The BMJ is published by the doctors' professional organisation (the BMA) so it will be well researched and reliable. This looks like a 'review' of recent research useful for healthcare practitioners. In the 'further' category.

On the reading list	What to expect?
Burden M (2003). Diabetes: signs, symptoms and making a diagnosis. *Nursing Times.* 99:1, 30–32.	A three-page article from a practitioner journal. Will be directly relevant to nursing practice. It looks 'core'.
Diabetes UK website: www.diabetes.org.uk/home.htm *Note:* This points you to a source, so does not include the details you would need to reference material from it.	A key and authoritative website in the field. Will contain a variety of material; probably good for current facts and figures (check dates of pages). Core.

Sustainable development module:

On the reading list	What to expect?
McGregor D (2002). Climate, environment and development. In Desai V and Potter RB (eds) *The companion to development studies.* London: Arnold.	A chapter in an edited book – itself on the reading list. Looks like a good intro. At a guess, 10–15 pages? Core.
UNFAO (2005). *Global forest resources assessment.* Available at http://www.fao.org/forestry/1191/en/ *Note:* Add the date you accessed it in your reference if you used it.	An authoritative website (United Nations). Will be a good source for up-to-date stats and trends. Core.

| Mather AS and Needle CL (2000). The relationship of population and forest land. *The Geographical Journal.* 166:1, 2–13. | An article (11 pages) of peer-reviewed[2] research.
Further. |

Feeling less panicky? At a closer look, reading lists often turn out to be less alarming than at first glance. The same text is referred to several times for different chapters; articles turn out to be really quite short; and careful use of good websites will take you to reader-friendly material, or at least well-structured sources where you can quickly find what you want.

Reading lists can point you to the debates

In every area of study, you will quickly find the topics of discussion or debate, on, for example:

▶ *the most appropriate way to treat this particular patient*
▶ *how best to protect forests*
▶ *how important the parent–parent relationship is in the early experiences of young children*

---

2 Every article in a 'peer reviewed' journal has been checked by specialists in the specific research area before publication.

In this example, a close reading of the reading list points directly to the debate at the heart of the essay task:

Essay question: *Do employees have real power in decision making?*

On the reading list	What to expect?
Argyris, C (1998). Empowerment: the Emperor's new clothes. *Harvard Business Review*. 76:3, 98–105.	An old source – a classic? The title suggests the author will argue that employees don't really have power. You'd have to read it to find out, and be ready to follow the argument …
Leathwaite, J (2005). Employee empowerment in service industries: a framework for analysis. *Personnel Development Journal*. 30:8, 768–83.	Looks like a more recent attempt to find a way to establish what the situation actually is. Could it be useful for a work-based assignment?
Rodriguez P and Watts R (2008). Decision-making and employee empowerment in the retail industry. *Management Studies*. 24:5, 648–60.	Focuses on one (key) aspect of empowerment in a major industry with large and small businesses.

Question taken from a Business Studies module: *Managing people*.

Can you spot the debates in your subject? If you can, it will help you focus your reading – and you will approach each source critically, looking for the 'position' of the author.

A critical search online

This section is about going beyond your reading list, beyond Google, or even Google Scholar. There is a huge world of research on just about everything under the sun out there at your fingertips. But how to find what you need, now? When you know what you are looking for (something closely related to a coursework topic, or your reading list), this is probably fairly straightforward – with a little help from your friendly library. But when you are thinking about a wide-open topic – such as a possible dissertation topic – you need to use databases, and get thinking. Critically of course, perhaps a bit like this:

You – the researcher

You're interested in carbon offsetting. It is a fairly recent area of research and there's not much on it in books. You follow the library handout on searching databases and …

???!!! Help! Where do I start? There's so much stuff …

Your friendly library ☺

SEARCH FOR

carbon offsetting

Search Results
1147 records for 1973–2013

Start thinking. What exactly do you want to explore in your dissertation? What question are you asking? This is far too general; it isn't asking a question and you can't research it. So focus down; narrow your field of interest. Ask a question.

I'm interested in deforestation too. I've seen wildlife programmes showing the impact. I'm interested in sub-Saharan Africa: so many problems that make survival so difficult for so many and here in the West even I can't resist a cheap flight …

So how about this for a question?
What is the effect of carbon offsetting on deforestation in sub-Saharan Africa?

Your friendly library ☺

SEARCH FOR

deforestation

AND   carbon offsetting

AND   sub-Saharan Africa

Search Results
0 records found

??!! Help! There's nothing on my topic!

No. There probably isn't. This is very specific. But before you give up, go and see your friendly subject librarian, who may help you find other sources, suggest other keywords. But if there really isn't anything? This could be great if you are engaged in original fieldwork research, but if you're not ...? You need to try a two-pronged approach. Think laterally! Critically!

First try locating research on an aspect of the issue I know is well established.

Your friendly library ☺
SEARCH FOR

deforestation

| AND | sub-Saharan Africa |

Search Results
17 records found ...

This is beginning to look researchable (migrant land rights / carbon storage in forestry / gorillas and armed conflict / cooking stoves ...) – but how to find out if there is a link with carbon offsetting?

There must be something on carbon offsetting AND deforestation in other parts of the world – or what's the debate about?

Your friendly library ☺
SEARCH FOR

deforestation

| AND | carbon offsetting |

Search Results
51 records found ...

... many relating to South America, South East Asia ... but might something here apply to sub-Saharan Africa? And if not why not? This is getting interesting ...

At this point you will be thinking critically about what you have found and making decisions about whether this precise topic is right for you, and whether this article is useful for your topic. It could be that it is not: it might be too unknown, perfect for a PhD student who is in a position to carry out research to fill a gap in knowledge – but not for you, now.

However, by finding out what research is out there, you may have stumbled across a topic that really grabs your interest, that relates to your previous general interest with a slight shift in focus, and that you can really engage with. Or you move up a level, and locate your question in the comfort zone in the middle. Only you can decide, but, having got this far, your decision will be based on sound – critical – thinking.

The research comfort zone

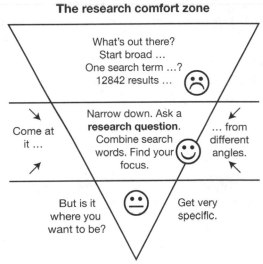

What's out there?
Start broad …
One search term …?
12842 results …

Come at it …

Narrow down. Ask a **research question**. Combine search words. Find your focus.

… from different angles.

But is it where you want to be?

Get very specific.

6 But is it any good? Evaluating your sources

'Evaluation' is something you do all the time, automatically. Look at what it means: see the word 'value' in the middle of '**evalu**ate'. It invites you to ask: what is the value of this? As research? As a source of information? To me, for my present purpose?

Any search online will throw up many more sources than you can possibly read or use. You need to develop ways of ruling them in or out so you only commit time and effort to the ones most likely to help you further understand your question.

This chapter focuses on the internet, because you'll be looking out there for sources for your assignment in the same way that you look for anything else. But it's not straightforward. The explosion of information we all have access to in a click means there are no gatekeepers to the quality of information around us, and we can move from high quality research to a random website, hardly noticing the switch. Today more than ever, the confidence to be 'critical' about any- and everything is perhaps *the* most important takeaway gain you will make in the course of your studies.

A critical look at the URL

As with a reading list, it helps to have an idea about an item before you go there. Look at the URL (the address) for clues. It gives an indication (but no more, since anyone can set up a company and country codes can be misleading) about the nature of the site.

While your fingers are tapping, get your brain thinking – critically! Your critical approach to web sources starts **before you leave the results page!**

The main part of the web address: company or organisation

a non-profit organisation

country where the organisation actually is

http://www.nice.org.uk/

What to expect	In the URL
Commercial organisation or company, big or small	.com (US or anywhere) or .co.uk (UK)
The country where the outfit is: France, Australia, UK, South Africa etc.	.fr .au .uk .sa etc.
A non-profit organisation	.org
Academic institutions	.edu (US) .ac.uk (UK)
A government agency	.gov

Then start your critical scanning before reading. Give yourself a framework by using a set of evaluation criteria – here the 'strategic questions'.

The strategic questions – again!

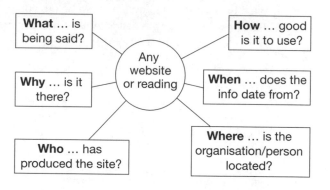

And overarching all these specific questions is the big one:

So what …?

So what … are the implications for other research in this area? … for future practice? Will I use this material in my assignment? How?

| **What** is being said? | **So what?** ... are the implications? |

- Fact? How do you know it's correct? Opinion? Whose? Argument? Based on what evidence?
- What evidence is there for statements/data?
- Does it show the sources of statements/data? References? Useful links?
- Is it the right level of detail for your purpose?
- Does the information here match with what you know already?
- Check it against a completely different source.

| **Why** is it there? | **So what?** ... are the implications? |

- What is the purpose or aim of the site or article? See 'About us' or similar.
- Why did they put this material up? To give access to information? Make research accessible? Promote debate? Explain? Persuade? Sell?

| **Who** has produced the site?/written the article/blog? | **So what?** ... are the implications? |

- An individual? organisation? Who are they? Can you contact them?
- How are they qualified to produce this material?
- Do they produce material in other formats – reports, books? Or link to other sites?
- Do other sources (like journals) use it?
- Has it been checked or reviewed by another expert?

How good is it to use?	**So what?** ... are the implications?

- User friendly? Starts from the perspective of a new user, not the webmaster?
- Logical, easy to navigate?

When does this information date from?	**So what?** ... are the implications?

- Does the material/data and its sources have dates?
- When was it last updated (see bottom of page)? If there is a date, use it for your reference.
- Is it kept maintained? Do the links work?

Where are they from?	**So what?** ... are the implications?

- Do they have a real address and telephone number? Check 'About us/Contact us'.

And remember why you are here!

You have to make a critical decision whether to move this material into your thinking about your question – or leave it out there …

7 To read or not to read? A critical decision

In searching databases (Chapter 5), you are on safer ground. All the articles you find will have been checked and reviewed by other experts in the field, and you can expect the research to be at least competent.

This does not mean, however, that everything you find will be relevant to you. Some results will be way off beam, hooked in by the different contexts of a keyword you used in your search (see *Planning Your Dissertation*, p. 49 for an example of this). Others may simply not be close enough to your focus to be worth reading.

You have **abstracts** to help you decide. These are short summaries of the article, often in about five sharply written sentences. Read this and then decide if the research looks so relevant to your topic or question that you want to read the full article.[3]

---

3 See 'How to read an abstract' and 'How to read an article' in *Planning Your Dissertation* in this series (pp. 51–2).

 GETTING CRITICAL

You find an article that looks promising, and here's the abstract. Use the strategic questions on p. 2 as a basic checklist to help you decide if it is worth reading the full text. A critical approach to reading – before you read – will save you a lot of time and effort.

Carbon offsets as an economic alternative to large-scale logging: a case study in Guyana

Tracey Osborne[a], 📄 ✉ and Clyde Kiker[b]

[a]Energy and Resources Group, University of California Berkeley, 310 Barrows Hall, Berkeley CA 94720, USA

[b]Food and Resource Economics Department, University of Florida, PO Box 110240, Gainesville, FL 32611, USA

Received 8 July 2002; revised 14 June 2004; accepted 18 June 2004. Available online 2 February 2005.

What is it about? A case study will be a detailed study in a particular setting.

Where was this research carried out? Could it have any relevance to my interest in Africa?

Who are the researchers? Do they look qualified to carry out credible research? Click on the icon to find out more about how the article has (or has not) been used by other researchers.

When was it published? (2005). When was the research carried out? (probably 2001-2).

Abstract

The objective of this study is to analyze the economic viability of carbon-offset projects that avoid logging in Guyana's forests. The results of this case study illustrate the cost effectiveness of alternative land-use options that reduce deforestation and associated greenhouse gas (GHG) emissions. This analysis demonstrates that using Guyana's rainforests for climate change mitigation can generate equivalent revenue to that of conventional large-scale logging without detrimental environmental impacts. At a 12% discount rate, the break-even price for carbon is estimated to be about US$ 0.20/tC. This estimate falls toward the low range of carbon prices for existing carbon offset projects that avoid deforestation.

Keywords: Carbon offsets; Deforestation; Climate change mitigation; Land use change and forestry; Guyana

Why was the research carried out? What is the aim?

What did they find out? And conclude?

How did they do it? You'd have to read the full article to find this out, and you would only do this if it is directly relevant to you.

So what ... are the wider implications of the research?

How might this research be useful to other projects? And of course to me. NOW?

Source: Reprinted from *Ecological Economics*, Volume 52, Issue 4 (1 March 2005), pp. 481–96 with permission from Elsevier.

OK. You decide that interesting though it is, it does not get close enough to your interest – which is shifting anyway towards one of the other related areas you came across earlier. So don't read it! Move on.

You're not a sponge taking it all in, reading from start to finish. As a critical reader, think of yourself as a hook, looking for relevant information to fish out, or a razor cutting through the details looking for the main points. It is your right, your decision, *not* to read – which is every bit as important as the decision to read!

When you do read, read economically – and critically, of course. Focus on the specific reading you have decided really is important and relevant to your research.

When you have identified a text you want to read in full, pause a moment. Don't dive ir and start from the beginning. This is a slow and inefficient way of reading.

Try the approach shown here to speed you up and target your time and effort.

First, look back at your assignment task or essay question:

....

Are you clearer now about your focus? And the sorts of materials you are looking for? (see *Planning Your Dissertation*, pp. 20–3 for examples of different sources you migh want to use).

Remind yourself … **Why** am I reading this text? **What** do I want to get out of it?

I want to …

Then get a feel for it …

1 Survey the text critically. Look at:

Title	Subtitle	Blurb	Author(s)	Date of publication	Contents (for overview) Index (for specifics)

2 Get an overview. Look for and skim:

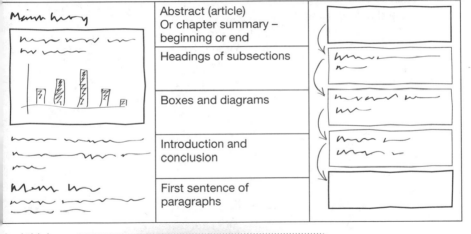

	Abstract (article) Or chapter summary – beginning or end
	Headings of subsections
	Boxes and diagrams
	Introduction and conclusion
	First sentence of paragraphs

And think:

How will this text help me with my topic?

This overview will enable you to see how the material is structured.

In a textbook chapter start with the
▶ chapter summary or
▶ first paragraph
▶ last paragraph
▶ headings and subheadings
▶ illustrative material – diagrams, boxes, charts, pictures.
… so you know where the key information is located for your detailed read.

In policy or government documents look to locate
▶ brief or terms of reference (who wanted the policy and why)
▶ aim and objectives
▶ specific policy relevant to your inquiry.
Then come back for the detailed reading of the specific sections.

In reports start with the
▶ abstract or executive summary
▶ introduction
▶ conclusions, maybe recommendations.
… and leave the Findings and Appendices for later (you may not need them).

In journal articles look at the

▶ abstract
▶ first paragraph / introduction (where the author sets out their perspective)
▶ last paragraph / conclusion (where the argument is restated, and linked to the wider issues)
▶ figures / data / boxes / diagrams.

To follow the line of reasoning in a text, read

▶ the abstract (for a short outline)
▶ introduction (the problem, approach, what lies ahead)
▶ conclusion (where the author gets to, how it fits in the wider picture)

and, before your detailed read,

▶ first sentence of paragraphs (for the step-by-step progression of their line of reasoning).

3 Any questions?

When you have an overview, you will know enough – and understand enough – about the text to know what you want to know more about. You will also know where to find it.

The next step is to note down these questions, or gaps you want to fill, before you go back to the text for your detailed read.

4 Detailed read

The detailed read will be easier now, as you have the sense of the whole, and can use the structure to guide your reading. You are able to focus on the key bits you have identified, and what you want to get out of it.

This strategic approach will speed up your reading, improve your comprehension and enable you to see where this particular text fits in the bigger picture of the question your are researching – a critical skill!

For more on reading strategies, see *Reading and Making Notes*, 2nd edn, in this series.

5 Record your research footprints

Keep track of your sources right from the start. If you don't use a source, you've lost nothing if you have the reference, but if you do want to use a source in your work, it is very frustrating to have to hunt for it again.

Your sources are incredibly important. They are your research footprints, the evidence for statements you make, the showcase for all the effort you put into your work, the basis of your critical thinking.

Look after them! Save the URL (of course), so you can find it again. However, the URL alone will not be sufficient to show your reader the quality of the sources you will be using.[4]

---

4 See *Referencing and Understanding Plagiarism* in this series for the details you need for a reference.

9 A critical record of reading

This chapter is about that point where you begin to engage with and make sense of your reading:

▶ in the **notes** you make (for yourself)
▶ in an **annotated bibliography** entry or post to be read by another person (tutor or student).

> *You will remember and understand notes you have written yourself.*
> *(RMIT 2013)*

Making notes

Note making from your reading is an incredibly important process. 'Process' is the right word, because it is when you make notes that your brain processes the information. It goes in as new information (data, explanation or argument), and down on your page as something you now know, understand, want to remember, and plan to use as you get to grips with your topic. You start off not knowing or understanding something, and end up knowing and understanding. That's great!

This is where you need to be careful. University education sets a high store by knowledge – which, if you like, is the core product of universities. An essential part of joining the academic community (which as a student you have done) is to be respectful of this knowledge (or argument, or explanation or whatever), and of the people who generated it or set it down. So record your sources meticulously.

Try to keep track of this separateness in your notes. Try to capture:

▶ the key points, key phrases of your source, and where it comes from
▶ your own thoughts, observations and connections. This is where you 'stand on the shoulders' of researchers and thinkers who have gone before.

Experiment with different formats for note taking till you find a way that works for you.

Tips for note making[5]	Why?
Record each source, the full reference, so you know where ideas or findings come from	▶ so your reader can find it ▶ to avoid retracing your steps later ▶ to get credit for the work you have done ▶ to give credit to authors for the work they have done.
Note key points relevant to your purpose	▶ to focus on what *you* want to get out of the text, not necessarily the same main points or order as the author.
Use colours, spacing, bullets, diagrams, arrows, sketches – whatever helps you understand the text. Go easy on the highlighter ... try a pencil.	▶ to change the format of the original to reflect how you are making sense of the information. A highlighter highlights – usually too much and you can't undo it!

Tips for note making[5]	Why?
Avoid writing full sentences	▶ to leave yourself free to grasp the idea, not get bogged down in the words of the writer.
Don't copy, except for short phrases you may want to use as quotes	▶ so the wording of your notes is your own except where you can see from the quote marks and page number that they are not.
Leave lots of space, and experiment with styles till you find what suits you	▶ so you can add detail later.
Check back quickly with the original	▶ to make sure you haven't missed anything crucial.

---

5 For more on making notes, see *Reading and Making Notes*, 2nd edn, in this series.

An annotated bibliography

An annotated bibliography may be set as a task (often at the midpoint of a bigger assignment) for a number of reasons. It may be to encourage you to:

▸ become familiar with finding and using research papers
▸ think critically about what you've read – to take you beyond repeating back what the article says
▸ gain confidence in writing about research in your own way, in your own 'voice'
▸ keep records of your research – your research footprints. It's surprisingly easy to forget what you've read!

> *Try thinking of it as 'futureproofing' (University of Cambridge, no date): leaving your future self clues for why you found it useful.*

The three-point structure overleaf – *summarise, evaluate, reflect* – helps you make the transition from understanding to evaluating, and reflecting critically on its implications for you and your work.

A short annotation: what do I include?

Read your guidance carefully! It should tell you what the tutor is looking for and give you an indication of length. In 100–150 words you can probably achieve the following. This structure also works for a longer critical review.

The full reference	
Summarise What is it about? (about 25% length)	▶ The author's purpose, aim or question ▶ Main argument, central idea, findings or conclusions ▶ What sort of text is it? General? Specific?
Evaluate What do I think about it? (about 50%)	▶ Who is it written for? ▶ Particular strengths or points of interest ▶ Similarities or differences with other things you have read, or ideas you hold yourself ▶ Any weaknesses or limitations?
Reflect How might I use it? (about 25%)	Has the text helped you understand something better? Or see/do something differently? If so, what? How useful is it? If so, how?

Don't overrun on the summary and slip into describing the text. Your lecturers may well know the text already, and are interested in *your* evaluation of strengths and limitations and *your* reflections on how it relates to your thinking and the assignment you are working on.

An example

Regina is researching an essay on the recruitment and retention of healthcare professionals in the NHS. Below is one annotation from her annotated bibliography.

Mills EJ, Schabas WA, Volmink J, Walker R, Ford N, Katabina E, Anema A, Joffres M, Cahn P and Montaner J (2008). Should active recruitment of health workers from sub-Saharan Africa be viewed as a crime? *The Lancet.* 371, Feb. 23, pp. 685–88.

Powerful argument – that wealthy countries contribute directly to worsening healthcare in poor sub-Saharan African countries, by actively recruiting h/c staff (doctors, nurses, pharmacists). Uses country-by-country WHO stats. Argues that it is unethical and contravenes various legal agreements.

Very readable, clearly and logically written, relevant to anyone interested in the negative impact of wealthy countries on poor countries today. Persuasive detail and good refs to wide range of sources (specific studies, international bodies, government and legal sources).

I was really shocked by the article, and hadn't been aware of this aspect of employing healthcare workers from other countries. May make this the focus of my essay, and need to research further.

You may even come to welcome having to write annotations! It gets you into the habit of standing back from what you have read, looking down on it and capturing what you thought of it. This is something you will develop the habit of doing anyway, as you become a more thoughtful – yes, critical – and confident student, leaving the sponge model of learning behind you.

As you find you know more, and understand better, ideas begin to take shape in your mind. If you look back to the 'stairway' on p. 14, you are now at the 'synthesis' point, when things start to come together.

You are ready to start planning your writing.

For another example of an annotation, see *Reflective Writing* in this series, pp. 61–2.

What does it say?
How are they different?
How do I use it?

Part 2 has tracked the pathway of a critical approach to reading and research. A critical approach isn't something you can switch on when you dive into a text. It starts where Part 2 starts – with thinking about what you know and what you need to know; and ends here, with thoughtful and critical analysis and evaluation of the materials you have read.

At this point you will be planning to draw it all together, to synthesise your learning, in order to answer the question you are working on.

On to Part 3!

GETTING CRITICAL IN WRITING

That point when you have completed the bulk of your reading and before you start writing is indeed 'critical'. It's essential – mission-critical – and it is the point at which you gain control of what you have read. You review your reading and notes, and start to work with it. It comes together as a synthesis.

It is 'synthesis with a purpose' because you have to use it in a particular way. You have to use it to 'answer' the question you have been set. The question is there to help you think critically, to stop you writing pages of all-I-know-about, to guide you in focusing and selecting, to draw your attention to conflicts of evidence, interpretation and argument in the topic area. It is your invitation to join the discussion.

Part 3 tracks this process.

10 Answer the question!

Look back to your strategic reading of your course handbook (pp. 3–5) and double-check that you have all the guidance you need to be crystal clear about what you have to do. Comments on returned work like these:

'So what does all this tell us about the question?'

'Why are you telling us about this?'

suggest that previously you have not kept the task in sharp focus throughout. This matters because a key way of showing your critical approach in your writing is by selecting only the materials and discussion that relate directly to the 'question' you have been asked.

But what if there isn't a question as such? If you were given a statement to write about or a broad topic to explore, how do you show your critical approach?

Look again. There is always a question in your title. It may be **explicit** (with a question mark) or it may be **implicit** in the instruction, or **hidden** in a bald title. You have to spot it, dig for it or create it. And then address it from start to finish.

Critical analysis in your writing starts here.

Getting critical with your 'question'

The explicit question

How far …? *How convincing is …?* *How successful …?* *Do you agree that …?* *In what ways …?* *What is the role of …?* *Can …?* **To what extent …?**	**The challenge here** is to pick the question apart, ask questions about it, and plan how to answer it. You show your critical approach by developing an argument, linking each point to one or other aspect of the question, and reaching a conclusion.
	The answer will usually be on a spectrum between 'Not at all' and 'yes totally'. If it were one of these extremes there would be little point in asking the question!

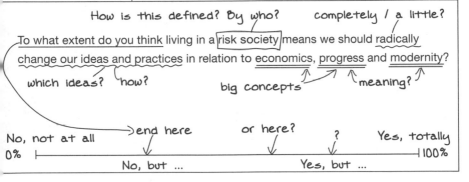

How is this defined? By who?   completely / a little?

To what extent do you think living in a risk society means we should radically change our ideas and practices in relation to economics, progress and modernity?

which ideas?   how?   big concepts   meaning?

No, not at all →end here   or here?   ?   Yes, totally
0%   No, but …   Yes, but …   100%

The instruction 'question'

Analyse the … *Compare and contrast the* *approaches to …* *Consider the impact of …* ***Discuss and evaluate …***	**The challenge here** is to appreciate what the 'instruction' word is asking for, and show your critical understanding of the topic by picking your way through the complexities. You show your critical awareness by doing exactly what it says!

'Assess the worth' and evidence

Different in what ways? Who holds these views? based on what?

What are they?

Discuss and evaluate <u>competing accounts</u> of <u>current</u> changes in the [role of nation-states] and the [prospects for global governance].

(1)

traditionally

(2)

future?

Conclude: where you end up in this discussion

The bald title 'question'

Future developments in the airline sector The equality and difference debate Going green: introducing an environmental management plan in the hotel industry	**The challenge here** is to create a structure for your essay by pulling out the headings hidden within the broad topic title, and picking out the debates within these specific areas. Show your critical understanding of these debates.

The Early Years Leader and change

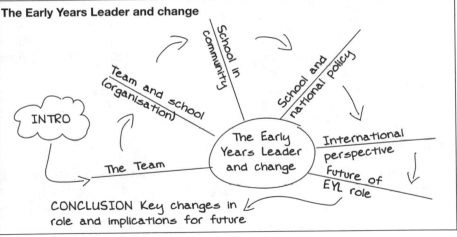

INTRO

School in community

Team and school (organisation)

School and national policy

The Early Years Leader and change

International perspective

The Team

Future of EYL role

CONCLUSION Key changes in role and implications for future

'Argument' in university writing

The guidance about essay structure given in school or college is often a good basis for your work at university. Use it as your point of departure, and be alert to the differences within that structure as you step up to university-level work.

At university, you build on this structure to show the angle you are taking. Of course you can only do this after you've done your reading and research and reflected on the evidence.

Your aim in writing an 'argument' essay at university is to convince your reader not only that you know what the arguments are, but that you understand them and see the 'weight' of each. You show that you can develop your own line of argument or 'position' in relation to the debate and bring it to a conclusion at the end.

Using structure to develop argument

The diagram opposite shows the structure of an argument essay. On the left is an outline of pre-university content, and on the right is an outline of the content expected at university. Each section of your essay does something more complex within the familiar structure.

Argument essay structure

Pre-university	Introduction	At university

Introduction
- Issues in the question
- *This essay ...*

Introduction
- Identify relevant issues in the question
- Explain what your argument will be
- *This essay ...* (main points)

Introduction

Issues in the question ...

This essay ...

...

Body
Arguments
- for
- against

Body

Body: your line of reasoning
- Set out main reasons for your argument
- Develop each reason in one paragraph
- Point out arguments against your line, and show why you think they are less convincing

Conclusion

Conclusion
- Which arguments you think are stronger

Conclusion
- Restate your argument
- Summarise what you covered
- Show what this means in relation to the question and the bigger picture

relating back to question

Thanks to Chara Bakalis (Senior Lecturer in Law, Oxford Brookes University) for her advice on argument in law essays at degree level.

This glimpse of some of the things you might be asked to do in an essay or assignment is to show how you are always being asked to 'answer' a 'question',[6] however it is phrased. You are never being asked to write-all-you-know-about. The 'critical' dimension runs throughout: in the skill in pinpointing the question, unpacking the question(s), setting the question yourself, and finding your 'position' in the debates or complexities in the topic. Finding your sense of direction or purpose through it all from start to finish is where your 'argument' lies. This is key to critical writing.

Your analysis of the question will point you to the research and reading you need to do. Then you can plan your answer in more detail, mapping out the points you want to address. You then move on to writing.

---

6 For more on how to analyse essay and assignment questions and plan your answer, see *Planning Your Essay* in this series.

Written work is divided into paragraphs. Mastering this basic unit of writing will give you the vehicle for showing your critical skills. The paragraph is in effect the unit of argument – each one is an interlocking link in your essay, leading to a conclusion.

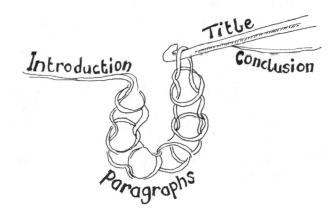

Here's why ... paragraphs are important

Paragraphs have a structure:

▶ A paragraph develops **one main idea**.

▶ This main idea is usually expressed clearly in one sentence, the first, or **'topic sentence'**.

▶ Paragraphs have a beginning, a middle and an end. The sentences in the middle explain, develop, illustrate or modify the main idea in the topic sentence. The last sentence often returns to the idea in the topic sentence to show how it has developed.

Paragraph structure has a purpose. It makes it easier to:

▶ **Read:** the main idea is first, and you know that this idea will be developed before you move on.

▶ **Plan:** each paragraph develops a single point. You can plan by mapping out the points.

▶ **Write:** new point, new paragraph. Start each paragraph with a clear statement of the point you are making, then add detail.

Here's how … to write a paragraph

All you need to write a paragraph is an idea of what you want to say, a point you want to put across. A paragraph is how you develop this idea into a short block of text, and your essay builds up paragraph by paragraph.

A paragraph plan

1 **Start with the topic sentence** to express the main idea.
2 **Explain or define any abstract, key or problematic terms** to clarify the topic sentence.
3 **Show your evidence** to support your main idea or argument in the topic sentence.
4 **Comment on the evidence** to show how it supports or develops the main idea. If appropriate, mention other evidence (examples/studies/experiments/interpretations) to widen the discussion.
5 **Conclude**. Look back to your topic sentence and ask yourself:
   ▸ how have I moved on/developed the main idea in it?
   ▸ where am I going next?
   ▸ Then write the last sentence.

Source: Williams (1995, pp. 45–47;1996, pp. 34–44). Many of the approaches and ideas in this guide – this section in particular – have developed from earlier publications on study skills.

Activity

Below is a paragraph from a student's essay. How does it match the paragraph plan? Try adding the numbers of the paragraph plan above to the text.

The Early Years Leader (EYL) needs to have an understanding of how teams work if they are to be effective in managing staff groups and change. An effective team will most likely go through stages of development (Hartley 1997). These stages have been described by Tuckman and Jensen (1977) as 'Forming' (a group gets to know each other), 'Storming' (some initial conflict develops), 'Norming' (group norms are established), 'Performing' (the group communicates and collaborates well) and 'Adjourning' (the group disbands). This cycle is repeated when new objectives are adopted or there is a change in team members, but to be able to perform to its optimum, a team needs to go through these stages to reach the 'performing' stage. It is the role of the Early Years Leader (EYL) to move the team through these stages trying to balance individual, professional and organisational needs and development.

1 The Early Years Leader (EYL) needs to have an understanding of how teams work if they are to be effective in managing staff groups and change. **2** An effective team will most likely go through stages of development (Hartley 1997). **3** These stages have been described by Tuckman and Jensen (1977) as 'Forming' (a group gets to know each other), 'Storming' (some initial conflict develops), 'Norming' (group norms are established), 'Performing' (the group communicates and collaborates well) and 'Adjourning' (the group disbands). **4** This cycle is repeated when new objectives are adopted or there is a change in team members, but to be able to perform to its optimum, a team needs to go through these stages to reach the 'performing' stage **4** It is the role of the Early Years Leader (EYL) to move the team through these stages trying to **5** balance individual, professional and organisational needs and development.

1. Topic sentence

2. Explain/define

3. Show your evidence

4. Comment

4. Comment

5. Conclude

DIY paragraph checking

Try checking the paragraph plan against:

▶ a paragraph of something you are reading;
▶ a paragraph you are writing.

Don't expect it to tally exactly, but you should be able to see a structure, with the topic sentence clearly stated at the beginning and elements of the 'plan' in the rest of the paragraph – even if it is just one or two words.

The paragraph plan and critical thinking

What happens when paragraphs don't follow this plan?

The *So what?* problem

You have main point, topic sentence (1), explanation (2), illustration, explanation, evidence (3):

> **1** The Early Years Leader (EYL) needs to have an understanding of how teams work if they are to be effective in managing staff groups and change. **2** An effective team will most likely go through stages of development (Hartley 1997). **3** These stages have been described by Tuckman and Jensen (1977) as 'Forming' (a group gets to know each other), 'Storming' (some initial conflict develops), 'Norming' (group norms are established), 'Performing' (the group communicates and collaborates well) and 'Adjourning' (the group disbands).

1. Topic sentence (main point)

2. Explanation

3. Illustration, explanation, evidence

But then you stop and move on to the next point in a new paragraph:

> The Early Years Foundation Stage places a great deal of emphasis on …

No Number 4. No comment from you, no evaluation, no evidence to the reader that you have understood what you have set out, no indication of how this evidence relates to the point you are making – and therefore no argument. The reader is left thinking 'So...?' Or '*But what does this tell us about …?*' or even **'So what?'**

The remedy

Make sure you have a Number 4: a comment on your 'evidence', however short.
In the example above the Number 4 comment peeps through in several phrases:

> This writer ...
> evaluates the usefulness of these
> ideas, picks out key aspects

4 This cycle is repeated when new objectives are adopted or there is a change in team members, but to be able to perform to its optimum, a team needs to go through these stages to reach the 'performing' stage. **4** It is the role of the Early Years Leader (EYL) to move the team through these stages trying to **5** balance individual, professional and organisational needs and development.

and links it back to
the topic sentence

applies the theory to
the situation

Other ways of showing you have a perspective on the material you discuss include:

- highlighting the differences between two studies
- showing you understand the points made, or the weight of argument, eg, 'key to this is ...' 'It seems that ...'
- connecting with the issues implicit in the question.

hese are a few of the ways of showing that you are on top of the material you have ead and are able to move around it, talking to your reader about the sense *you* make f it. In short, in your Number 4 you show your critical awareness of what you are vriting about.

Key point: Answer the 'So what?' question before your reader has time to ask it! Make your comments.

ow long is a paragraph?

low long is a piece of string? Long enough to do what you want it to? Or not? The ame applies to paragraphs. A paragraph needs to be long enough to develop a point r idea in the way outlined in the paragraph plan.

or the academic writing of most students 5–8 sentences is a good guideline. Are you vithin this range? Try the upside down test.

he upside down test

urn your essay or assignment upside down and turn the pages. Does it look inviting o read?

Satisfying customers should be the overriding aim of marketing activity. To what extent does this (literature?)

This definition covers the important point that the needs and objectives of both the customer and the organisation must be satisfied. Satisfying customers should be an essential part of marketing activity for it is a chapter to satisfy and thereby retain existing customers than it is to attract new. According to Macنamara et al (2004) it costs approximately five times more to attract a new customer than to retain existing customers happily. Commonly it needs to be considered that it does to keep an existing customer happily. Commonly it needs to be considered that more existing a customer base and all pursues will be profitable to the company. In retail banking for example, the definition covers the important point that the needs and objectives of both the customer...

This big block of text is most off-putting. It also tells your reader that you have not structured your argument into separate points, and you blur everything together.

The remedy? Read through carefully, spotting when you move onto a new point, and make this a new paragraph. Check you have clear topic sentences.

Satisfying customers should be the overriding aim of marketing activity. To what extent does this

This definition covers the important point that the needs and objectives of both the customer and the organisation must be satisfied. Satisfying customers should be an essential part of marketing activity for it is a chapter to satisfy and thereby retain existing customers than it is to attract new (Oliver 1999). According to Macنamara et al (2004) it costs approximately five times more to attract a new customer than to retain existing customers happily.

This is off-putting too. Your reader will assume that you have a 'shopping list' approach to points and ideas. You can't develop a point properly in one or two sentences.

The remedy? It may be that some of your mini-bites belong together. Run them together to form a paragraph. Or it may be that you have lots of points, each a topic sentence in itself. Try using the paragraph plan to develop each point.

Satisfying customers should be the overriding aim of marketing activity. To what extent does the literature?

This definition covers the important point that the needs and objectives of both the customer and the organisation must be satisfied. Satisfying customers should be an essential part of marketing activity for it is cheaper to satisfy and thereby retain existing customers than it is to obtain new ones (Oliver 1999). According to Masterson et al (2006) it costs approximately five times more to attract new customers that it does to keep an existing customer happy. Conversely it needs to be considered that even within a customer base not all patrons will be profitable to the company. In retail banking for example, the This definition covers the important point that the needs and objectives of both the customer and the organisation

Must be satisfied. Satisfying customers should be an essential part of marketing activity for it is cheaper to satisfy and thereby retain existing customers than it is to obtain new ones (Oliver 1999). According to Masterson et al (2006) it costs approximately five times more to attract new customers that it does to keep an existing customer happy. Conversely it needs to be considered that even within a customer base not all patrons will be profitable to the company. In retail banking for example, the This definition covers the important point that the needs and objectives of both the customer and the organisation must be satisfied. Satisfying customers should be an essential part of marketing activity for it is cheaper to satisfy and thereby retain existing customers than it is to obtain new ones (Oliver 1999). According to Masterson at al (2006) it costs approximately

Five times more to attract new customers that it does to keep an existing customer happy. Conversely it needs to be considered that even within a customer base not all patrons will be profitable to the company. In retail banking for example, the This definition covers the important that the needs and objectives of both the customer and the organisation must be satisfied. Satisfying customers should be an essential part of marketing activity for it is cheaper to satisfy and thereby retain existing customers than it is to obtain new ones (Oliver 1999). According to Masterson et al (2006) it costs approximately five times more to attract new customers that it does to keep an existing customer happy. Conversely it needs to be considered that even within a customer base not all patrons will be profitable to the company.

This definition covers the important point that the needs and objectives of both the customer and the organisation must be satisfied. Satisfying customers should be an essential part of marketing activity for it is cheaper to satisfy and thereby retain existing customers than it is to obtain new. it does to keep an existing customer happy. Conversely it needs to be considered that even within a customer.

page of writing should look something like this – this time the right way up, with aragraphs moving down the page looking like they are long enough to develop an dea, but not so long that they merge ideas or ramble.

This is very rough and ready – allow for differences in line spacing, variation between different sections of your essay, the norms in different subject areas – but use these images as a jog to check your paragraphing.

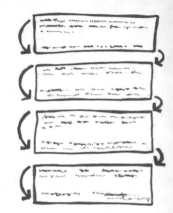

Well-structured paragraphs are an essential tool in demonstrating your ability to see key points and to set out a coherent argument or account that flows from one point to the next. These qualities are fundamental to critical thinking, analysis and writing.

Chapter 12 is about critical writing. The main character in this chapter is the reader – a critical reader, your lecturer or tutor, the person who assesses your work. This reader knows what they are looking for in their students' writing and they have given you clues as to what it is.

In Chapter 2, you saw these expressed as qualities in the assessment criteria. These are what your critical reader is looking for. The problem for many students, however, is knowing what these abstract qualities look like in writing on the page. This chapter aims to show you this through examples of student writing and tutor comment.

'Tell me more …'

First, let's take a look at writing that leaves a reader thinking something like: *Where are you in all this? Where is your voice, your comment, your understanding of why it matters? Tell me more …*

Below are extracts from the first draft of essays and assignments by several students. The comments on the right are the sort a critical but friendly reader might make to help these writers to develop their own 'voice' and to show their critical awareness of what they are writing. *For your redraft* gives specific feedback the student can use for their final draft.

Critical writing 1: 'Evidence ...?' Show your evidence

> Even though women have a guaranteed job, after maternity leave they often find themselves competing against their replacement on their return.

For your redraft: Check you have good evidence for this comment. If not, take it out – it may not be essential to your wider argument.

A critical thinker will make sure their statements are based on **evidence** the reader can check.

A tutor may write 'Evidence??' in the margin. I'd like to know how you know this. Common sense? Personal experience? Neither of these are the sorts of evidence you need to support an assertion like this.

Critical writing 2: 'Not a credible source ...' Use reliable sources

> Men are often considered to be more computer literate, which enables them to understand and do things at a faster rate than women (Donoghue 2007).

For your redraft: Think hard about whether this is a point that helps your overall argument. If you still want to make it, do more extensive research to satisfy yourself as to whether there is good evidence for your statement.

A critical thinker will **ask questions** about the quality of their sources, and not use material with weak evidence.

Tutor comment: 'Not a credible source'. Every reader will want to check your source for this (contentious) statement! Your reference shows that it was 'Travel Weekly', which is not a reliable source for a statement like this! It won't be based on high quality research.

Critical writing 3: 'So ...?' Apply your understanding

Letbridge (1997) argues that communication skills support and pervade the whole concept of working in partnership. Moreover, professionals are less effective on their service users' behalf if they cannot communicate precisely and persuasively (Lodge 2000). Stanley (2003) comments that to ...

For your redraft: Take a deep breath and talk to your reader. Explain the implications of these observations for work with clients.

Letbridge (1997) argues that communication skills support and pervade the whole concept of working in partnership. **In a multidisciplinary team ...** Lodge (2000) **observes that** professionals are less effective on their service users' behalf if they cannot communicate precisely and persuasively. **In care settings where staff come from many cultural backgrounds, language is ...** Stanley (2003) comments that to ...

A **critical thinker** will **apply** their reading to their situation, not just describe it.

A tutor might think 'So ...??' I can see you have read widely and summarise key points well, but where are you going with it? How does this relate to practice?

Deepen your discussion by showing how the point applies in a practical context.

Introduce your source as soon as you start to discuss their point.

Don't let this important point slide by! Add your comment to show how it applies in practice.

Critical writing 4: *Quote hopping!* Tell us why the quote is important

Bowlby's theory of attachment showed that 'the infant and young child should experience a warm, intimate and continuous relationship with his mother or mother substitute .' (1982 p11). Rutter (1981) found 'the child is more likely to develop deviant behaviour' (p18) …

For your redraft: Do some thinking. Explain the differences between these writers in your own words. Too many quotes makes your writing disjointed, and the reader can't see what interests you in the discussion. Cut down on the quotes drastically.

In his theory of attachment, Bowlby (1982) stressed the importance of a 'warm, intimate and continuous' relationship (p11) with an adult. He did not insist that this should be the mother. It could be a 'mother substitute'. This is important in any discussion of the role of parents and carers in the development of young children …. Rutter (1981) focused on what happens when this relationship is disrupted … Neither argued that the mother should be the exclusive carer …

A **critical thinker** will draw sources together, linking them to their interest and discussion. They will only **quote** key, special words, and then **comment**, making sure that their own voice comes through.

A tutor might think: where are you going with this? You hop from quote to quote describing what each writer says. Don't be nervous about summarising and commenting on theories and findings. Your voice is missing.

In her first draft Eva hadn't shown what interests her in this debate: the roles of mother and carer.

Summary and comment.

A glimpse of Eva's argument …

Synthesis linking two sources.

Eva's focus, Eva's voice

Do use feedback!

The comments on each extract offer the student a lot of feedback. You may not get advice as specific as this, but you will get some feedback about the effective and less effective aspects of your writing.

Positive feedback often comes in the form of a tick on your text – no more! Look back at marked essays, working out why you got each tick: a good use of example; a well-observed point; good use of a reference; intelligent application of a point from research to a particular situation …

Look closely at marginal comments:

*This is a **jargon term** if you don't explain or reference it*

*What are the **implications** for …?*

*Link your discussion of **policy** to the topic …*

While these are highly specific comments on one (very good) essay, the points in bold indicate issues this student is likely to encounter again, and can learn from. If you look at several essays, you may see a pattern emerging – what needs to be on your personal hit list? If you can do this in a group with other students, all taking the approach 'we need to understand the feedback' (not being negative or personal), you could all learn a lot.

Becoming a critical writer: takeaway points

To become a critical thinker (and so a writer), be prepared to challenge yourself. Come back to your first draft after a break (ideally of several days), and you will be better able to see it with fresh eyes.

As a critical reader of your own writing, try to:

> - **Ask questions:** you could start with the strategic questions, and adapt them.
> - Look for **evidence** for statements or assertions.
> - Check for **assumptions and personal views** with no wider basis in evidence.
> - Check for sweeping statements and **generalisations** – a comment that may be true of one situation but not true when applied to others.
> - Probe the **knowledge** base of the writing – superficial or in-depth? Do you really understand it? (If you don't as a writer, your reader certainly won't!)
> - Find your **voice** as a writer. *Tell me why it matters or how it is different. Explain the implications, applications, uses. Talk to me, your reader.*

So what *are* tutors looking for?

The language tutors use in feedback on first-class work is revealing. It reminds you of what they are looking for, and what they have found: *(critical) analysis ... argument ... debates ... evidence ...* It is the language of assessment (Chapter 2), successfully achieved.

> *You have considered several issues arising from the relevant literature and you have explained and analysed them ...*

> *Good discussion of theoretical concepts. Excellent use of supporting evidence to illustrate arguments.*

> *Well referenced, using articles from the reading list plus other relevant sources including relevant peer-reviewed articles.*

> *Argument is succinctly and unequivocally stated in the introduction.*

> *This essay shows a high level of knowledge and understanding of the debates and advances a coherent and convincing argument.*

> *You have identified all the relevant debates and theories surrounding this subject. Your critical analysis is of a high standard ...*

> *You have read extensively and use the empirical evidence that you have found to support your arguments, and in your analysis ...*

What does 'critical' writing look like?

The extracts from first-class student essays and assignments below show what these qualities look like on the page. The comments point out features of good writing (including the paragraph plan, p. 63) and link to the 'Stairway to critical thinking' (p. 14 and Chapter 14).

Extract 1

Although empowerment is a management initiative, this does not necessarily mean that empowerment is not of benefit to employees. Hertzberg's two-factor theory of motivation at work (Hertzberg et al. 1959 cited in Mullins 1998) clearly shows that responsibility and recognition are motivators that lead to job satisfaction. The problem is that not all employees can be categorised under Herzberg's framework. Many employees only work to earn money. Argyris (1998) label these as 'externally committed' (p89). When trying to empower staff, these are the people that …

A thoughtful, critical comment in the topic sentence, direct from the writer: critical analysis.

This short summary from a key source shows the writer has understood, and selected only the key point needed for their discussion.

A 'no. 4' comment (from paragraph plan)! The writer's own comment, identifying the limitations of this theory, and moving swiftly to explore the theory of another author: critical analysis.

Good synthesis linking ideas and theories in a discussion.

Extract 2

There is considerable consensus about the impact of early experience, although there have been some dissenting voices. These include Harris (1998), who questioned the extent of parental influence, and considered the influence of peers to be greater. This, however, is unlikely to be the case in the first few years of life. Kagan (1998) has been a strong opponent of the notion of 'infant determinism' (p62), and ...

A clear topic sentence, making the writer's point for the paragraph, and indicating wide reading in order to be able to say this – with authority: introducing evidence.

A short, sharp summary showing the writer's understanding of these authors.

A 'Number 4' comment! The writer has reflected on the theory and made a brief comment of their own before moving on to the next theorist: synthesis.

Extract 3

... In this essay I argue that it is not possible to solve global environmental problems within the structure of the global political economy because the principles which underpin the competitive free market unavoidably exploit the environment. However ... it is important to consider what intervention in the global economy might involve, and what it might achieve.[7]

To set out an argument so clearly in the introduction, the writer must have read and thought a lot before they begin. Issues are never black or white. This writer will pick their way carefully, setting out their line of reasoning, and consider conflicting evidence. The conclusion will show where they sit in the debate and why.

The writer uses language carefully and critically. Not 'solve' but it might 'achieve' something.

7 For more on language, see *Writing for University* in this series.

Your perspective, your argument

One word in the tutor feedback (p. 79) recurs more than any other: **argument.** Let's take a closer look at what 'argument' means, and how you develop argument in your written work. Start, of course, by analysing the question.

Can ...? Do ...? **Should ...?**	**The challenge here**, in a short, direct question on a contentious issue, is to see how much lies beneath the surface. The question may look simple, but you need to pick at it and draw out the content and debates – as with the explicit question on p. 55 .

> Yes? No? Arguments both ways will be strong.
>
> Moral?
> Legal?
>
> All prisoners? Some?
>
> *Should* | prisoners | have the <u>right</u> to <u>vote?</u>
>
> Who or what grants rights?
> Parliament? European Court of HR?
>
> Significance in a democratic society?
>
> CONCLUSION: of <u>your</u> argument

This analysis will give you some starting points – so will your course material. Your research will take you to:

▶ core knowledge (human rights, legal rulings)
▶ perspectives you may not have thought of (features of a democratic society)
▶ the debate you now join.

Do the groundwork: what are the arguments?

FOR	AGAINST
▶ ECHR[8] says prisoners should retain basic human rights (including the right to vote)	▶ Loss of vote a deterrent to future offending – part of the punishment
▶ Linking ban to imprisonment is arbitrary – what if someone is in for a short time?	▶ Prisoners should experience the 'civic death': they've acted against the interests of society
▶ Right to vote helps prisoners to reintegrate eventually into society	▶ Losing the right to vote will help prisoners rehabilitate, and regret their decisions
▶ Prisoners' views should be represented in Parliament	▶ Prisoners can't be trusted to make good political decisions

Which set of arguments do you find more convincing? If this is the first time you've thought about the issue, you are probably just expressing your opinion. But if you dig deeper (as a law student, for example) you will see the depth of the arguments. Your **evaluation** of the evidence (see p. 105) will lead you to formulate your perspective, your argument.

This reflection and hard thinking will ensure you develop your own perspective. Your challenge in writing the essay is to convince your reader that your argument is valid and well evidenced.

---

8 European Court of Human Rights

Different arguments, different essays

Should prisoners have the right to vote?

Essay 1

Introduction
- The debate: involves different views about punishment
- *This essay argues that denying voting rights should form no part of punishment ...*

Body: arguments
- Will it rehabilitate? No, because ...
- Prison is punishment enough ... no need to deny all human rights
- Crime is complex ... link to social and economic factors ...

Conclusion
No good reason to deny prisoners the vote ... not to be decided by 'popular punitiveness' ...

Essay 2

Introduction
- Prisoners have broken the law ...
- *This essay argues that prisoners should not have the right to vote: 'civic death'*

Body: arguments
- Loss of participation in society should include loss of right to vote: a 'privilege' not a 'right'
- Human rights are not clear cut
- A deterrent ...
- What about the victims?

Conclusion
Good reasons for not giving prisoners the right to vote; Parliament can ignore the ECHR.

Essay 3

Introduction
- Good arguments for and against – a complex issue
- *This essay will argue in favour of the right to vote, but only to an extent ...*

Body: arguments
- Strength of the argument depends on crime committed ...
- Human rights not absolute ...
- Different approach: allow the vote but take it away for serious crimes. This meets the ECHR ruling ...

Conclusion
Not a simple issue: thinking needs to focus on best fit for individual and society ...

Thanks to Chara Bakalis (Senior Lecturer in Law, Oxford Brookes University) for her kind permission to include this adaptation of her teaching materials.

There is no 'right' answer, of course; there will be many different perspectives in the pile of essays the tutor marks. Perhaps you are beginning to be persuaded by one argument over the others, or at least to see the complexity of the issues that each of these essays considers.

The language of argument

The language used in argument is always carefully chosen. The final draft of a successful piece of work is the outcome of careful editing and checking to make sure you say exactly what you meant to say. Consider these points.

Consider ...	Try this
Have you overstated? Gone beyond what you meant, been too definite?	Choose words that convey the right degree of certainty for the point you are making. Consider the impact of (for example): *has been described as / may be / likely to / can / can be seen as / implies that / does not necessarily mean that /*

Consider ...	Try this
Does your writing flow? Do you make it easy for your reader to follow your argument?	Use 'signposting' or linking words to help your reader: ▶ follow the flow of your argument: *first(ly); second(ly) / next /* ▶ see the connections between ideas and anticipate the direction you are going in: *however / therefore / so / for example.* These are examples of words you can use to help your reader follow your flow.[9]
Do the words you use to introduce a source show your 'position' on the author and the issue?	Choose your verb carefully when you summarise a point from a source: *points out / argues / maintains / claims / concludes / suggests* These words – and many many others[10] – tell your reader not just that you have read the source, but that you have developed a position in relation to it.

See *Planning Your Dissertation* (Chapter 19) in this series.

Part 3 has taken a look at the key processes that underpin effective and convincing critical writing. The main tool used to do this is – of course – analysis: analysis of the question; of argument; in writing. As you develop skills of analysis, you will become a critical, questioning and confident student.

---

9 For more on language in writing, see *Writing for University* (Chapter 17) in this series.
10 These examples are a few of many in the excellent University of Manchester Academic Phrasebank.

CRITICAL STEPS

Part 4 is about the next – critical – steps in developing and using the skills of analysis.

Chapter 13 shows how a 'framework' can be used as a 'tool' to help with critical analysis of a problem, situation or process.

Chapter 14 returns to the 'stairway to critical thinking' (see p. 14) to take a closer look at what you can do with your analysis of an issue, situation or problem. It shows what is involved in those processes further up the stairway, when you synthesise, evaluate, apply, justify.

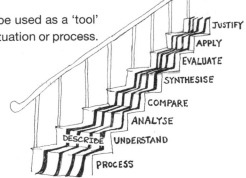

Thinking up models to explain and interpret the world around us – or at least that bit we are engaged in studying – is a fundamental analytical response to being alive and thinking. There are a few models in this guide already:

▶ the 'stairway' to critical thinking (of course!) (p.14, Ch. 14)
▶ the research comfort zone triangle (p. 27)
▶ the mention of the dynamic of group processes (p. 64)
▶ and see also *Reflective Writing* in this series. Part 4 outlines several frameworks used for critical analysis of a problem, situation or experience and the reflections that arise from this analysis.

'Model' and 'framework' are both terms for thinking structures that people have developed to help critical analysis. If you are asked to use a 'framework' in an analysis, what is it you are being asked to do?

About frameworks

Whatever issues you are considering, you are not the first person ever to do so. You are building on work that has gone before, by other people who have been there before.

These researchers have not necessarily had exactly the same experiences or thoughts in exactly the same contexts, but they have been in similar situations, researched and reflected on them, and developed a way of categorising characteristics, or looking at a situation that may be helpful to other people – you, for example.

Using a framework can help you:

▸ see different aspects or elements more clearly – easy to lose in the muddle of reality or the whirl of ideas or conflicting approaches. This is 'analysis'.

▸ pick out key themes or aspects, and stop you telling the story of what you did, read or thought. This avoids 'description'.

▸ make changes in what you do: to step up from anecdote and adopt a more systematic or better justified basis for actions. This is 'application'.

Frameworks can help you to think critically, by giving you some fixed points for doing your basic analysis, on which you can then build your own interpretations, reflections and applications.

See the difference when you add a picture frame to a sketch! It goes from being just something that's happening to something you stand back and look at and reflect on.

This section illustrates this with a brief look at a few well-used frameworks.

Using a framework for analysis: SWOT

This model is most often used in business-related subjects, but it is also used in a wide range of contexts: for example, by a GP practice on a training day, or by people considering career options.

Here you are asked to consider the internal **S**trengths and **W**eaknesses of an organisation (usually), and the **O**pportunities and **T**hreats it faces externally (hence SWOT).

Internal factors **Looking *in*** (to yourself, an organisation) what are your/their …	**External factors** **Looking *out*** (to the external environment in which you or the organisation is operating) what are the …
STRENGTHS	OPPORTUNITIES
WEAKNESSES	THREATS

Only after you have completed the analysis do you consider what you DO next, with a critical discussion of the options, hopefully leading to an action plan (for yourself or to recommend to an organisation).

Try it!

On yourself: considering a career move.

Looking *in*	Looking *out*
STRENGTHS What are you good at? What do you enjoy? **WEAKNESSES** What do you struggle with?	**OPPORTUNITIES** What's out there that could use what you're good at? And your enthusiasm? **THREATS** What could limit you? Developments on the horizon that make it more difficult?

An analysis using fixed points like these SWOT analyses helps you distance yourself from the 'story' or case study, and become analytical. You pick out key points and allocate them to different headings in a systematic way. As a 'tool' it will usually go in the appendix. So what goes in your text? Your critical discussion informed by your reading and other sources of ideas as you compare, contrast, evaluate, justify – or do whatever you have been asked to on the basis of this underpinning analysis.

On an organisation: to evaluate its position or effectiveness.

Typical general questions are shown first. Key points from a student's SWOT analysis of a restaurant is shown in small bullet points.

Looking *in*	Looking *out*
STRENGTHS What are they successful at? Do well? ▶ Good local reputation ▶ Good location (wealthy village and on high street) ▶ Fairly well trained staff and low turnover ▶ Locally sourced food	**OPPORTUNITIES** How could they use their strengths to achieve something extra? ▶ Closure of L'Orangerie restaurant in March ▶ Growing customer interest in local food ▶ Trend away from brands
WEAKNESSES What lets them down, or risks letting them down in terms of (for example) staff or systems or purpose? ▶ Limited parking ▶ Old property (small kitchen) ▶ No online booking ▶ Little promotion	**THREATS** What external factors or developments could impact negatively? ▶ Economic downturn – esp on classier dining out ▶ Opening of Piazza brasserie in June ▶ Dependent on access by car/petrol costs

Combining frameworks

You can use two or more models or frameworks to analyse a situation, in a complementary way. Here is an example.

Group development and team roles

Students are sometimes asked to write a 'reflective account' or a 'critical reflection' on the process of their group in working towards the eventual product – a poster, report or whatever. Here it is very easy to become descriptive, telling the story of the process: *x did this, y said that, we all thought* ... etc. This is not what is required.

You are being asked to relate your experience of the pleasures and pitfalls of working in a group to the research, thinking and reflection of others who have been there before – just as with any other 'framework'. The challenge is to relate theory to practice, which can feel difficult when what you are doing seems so everyday and routine. This is where a framework is useful. Try this approach as a starting point.

First, analyse the overall progress of your group towards the end product, using the framework mentioned in the paragraph on p. 64. Use the headings for your analysis.

Framework 1: Stages of group development

Forming	A group of people gets together, by choice or allocation.
Storming	Differences of view or approach emerge and conflict arises.
Norming	The group sets to work, and takes on roles and tasks.
Performing	The group works well and delivers.
Adjourning	The group completes its task and disbands.

Source: Boddy (2008, pp. 570–72). This text is one of many that discuss and develop the original model by Tuckman and Jensen (1977).

Not that it will feel like this! And not all groups get through all the stages. Whatever the outcome, it is your task to analyse what is going on, for better or worse. To what extent was it similar to the process outlined in this model? And in what ways was it different? An account that develops from this sort of analysis, comparing the theory with the practice, will have a critical dimension.

You could combine this consideration of the overall process of the group with an analysis of the roles of each individual.

Framework 2: Team roles

Many thinkers have analysed the working of teams or groups in terms of the role or roles each individual takes on and how they interact. Belbin (1993) researched team interactions and came up with this model.

Belbin's nine team roles:

1	**Plant:** creative, imaginative, unorthodox	6	**Teamworker:** cooperative, mild, perceptive and diplomatic
2	**Resource investigator:** extrovert, enthusiastic, communicative	7	**Implementer:** disciplined, reliable, conservative, efficient
3	**Coordinator:** mature, confident, a good chairperson	8	**Completer:** painstaking, conscientious, anxious
4	**Shaper:** challenging, dynamic, thrives on pressure	9	**Specialist:** single-minded, self-starting, dedicated
5	**Monitor–evaluator:** sober, strategic, discerning		

Source: Belbin (1993). This short extract only gives the role name and description of characteristics.

You can use the profiles as a starting point for analysing the roles of your actual team members, and write a critical account of how they interact in the course of carrying out the task set. In a group of, say, four people, each person will combine roles, and they may well overlap and change. Again, it lifts you out of any temptation to tell the story of the group, and offers a basis for analysis and critical thinking.

Developing frameworks

Frameworks develop. They are organic, part of the intellectual process on which research is based. Researchers are often described as 'standing on the shoulders of giants', with new discoveries and developments and ways of thinking building on what went before. This is the core business of research and critical thinking.

You may find yourself feeling that the framework you are using does not quite work for you. Clearly Boddy (2008) did. He discusses both the frameworks outlined above and develops and amends them. He also gives the reference to the original work so the reader can track the original framework and use it if they prefer – which I did with Belbin.

Here are some more examples:

The 'Stairway to critical thinking' (Open University 2008)	I have developed this in this guide to show the text as a staircase, with one process building on the next.
Group development (Tuckman and Jensen 1977)	Maureen Guirdham (2002) has developed this to show how the focus on individual, group and task needs changes through the stages. Interesting.
A SWOT analysis is often combined with a PEST analysis in business (Political, Economic, Social, Technical) in analysing the opportunities and threats in the external environment …	… to which a final E – for 'Ecological' – has been added in recent years to reflect the growing importance of this aspect.

… and so on.

Getting critical with a framework

If you decide to amend an existing framework, you are in good company, part of the mainstream of academic evolution. It will be the outcome of some hard critical thinking. You have to justify the changes you want to make, showing the strengths of the particular framework and its uses, but also its limitations as a tool for the analysis you want to make. Part of your justification will come from other things you have read, and you will need to show the basis for the changes you want to make in the same way as you need to show the evidence for any other point or argument.

You can, of course, develop your own framework … and if you decide to do this you are flying beyond the scope of this guide! Enjoy!

14 Stepping up the stairway to critical thinking

Describe

DESCRIBE	Understand	Comprehend the key points, assumptions, arguments and evidence presented.
Process	Take in the information, i.e. what you have read, heard, seen or done.		

Students often worry that their work is 'descriptive' not 'analytical', and tutors' comments often underline this. To be able to 'describe' is an essential first step. As the 'stairway' suggests, you need to take in (or 'process') information, and make sure you understand it. Describing is, however, only a first step and at university you are usually expected to go beyond this.

But how do I know I'm describing?

If you feel you have to keep going to tell the story (an account, case study, observation), panicking because you've written four pages and only just got to … and there is so much more … up hill and down dale …

… then you are describing: *what this and that writer said/practitioner did/you observed.*

The remedy?

STOP!
Step back! Get a perspective …
Step up to analysis.

Analyse

Analysis is defined as 'the resolution of something complex into its simple elements' (*Shorter Oxford English Dictionary,* 1983).

Analysis is the foundation to critical thinking.

	Analyse	Examine how these key components fit together and relate to each other.

The lowly place of analysis on the stairway underplays its crucial importance. Analysis is the springboard to critical thinking because until you can see the 'key components' and how they 'fit together', you can't think about them, manipulate them, work out their merits or use them.

To step up to analysis, leave description behind. Stop the narrative, stop telling the story. Stand up for a moment! Look down on the situation, see the themes emerging from the 'story'. Pick out key points that relate to each other and to the question or task you are working on.

Then replan your work by theme.

Compare (and contrast)

The instruction 'Compare and contrast' leads to analysis of themes that emerge from the groundwork analysis of similarities and differences.

	Compare	Explore the similarities and differences between the ideas you are reading about.

If you are asked to 'compare', you will also 'contrast'. In things that are very different, the similarities are interesting. In things that are very similar, the differences are more interesting. So inevitably you do both (to a greater or lesser extent) when you are asked to do either.

The analysis becomes interesting when you start to explore the implications of the similarities and differences you have identified: why they are important; what they mean. As you distance yourself from the detail, you will see themes emerging. These are the themes you structure your essay around. Something like this:

Step 2: Identify the themes: analyse and discuss

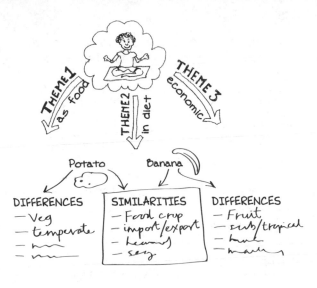

Step 1: Do the groundwork: list similarities and differences
START HERE

THEME 1 as food

THEME 2 in diet

THEME 3 economic

Potato

Banana

DIFFERENCES
- Veg
- temperate
- ~~
- ~~

SIMILARITIES
- Food crop
- import/export
- ~~~
- ~~

DIFFERENCES
- Fruit
- sub/tropical
- ~~
- ~~

Planning Your Essay, p. 60, in this series has a useful diagram to help with this analysis.

Synthesise

Synthesis is another powerhouse process. It's what you do when you have completed your reading and research on a topic and start to make sense of it.

Bring together different sources of information to serve an argument or idea you are constructing. Make logical connections between the different sources that help you shape and support your ideas.	**Synthesise**	

Synthesis is when you put together your thoughts with the evidence and thoughts that arise from your reading and research. You plan your writing to make sure your reading will 'serve' the points you want to make. In making 'logical connections' between different sources, you may point out differences, reservations and agreement between your sources. You show your critical approach in the comments you make about your sources (remember Number 4 in the paragraph plan? p. 63) and in the language you use.

By this process you can develop your line of reasoning through your sources and show your perspective on an issue.[11]

---

11 For more on the language of argument, see *Planning Your Dissertation*, Ch. 19, in this series.

Evaluate

Assess the worth of an idea in terms of its relevance to your needs, the evidence on which it is based and how it relates to other pertinent ideas.	**Evaluate**	

You've thought about the relationship between ideas and interpretations; now you look more carefully at each one to consider its merits, its strengths and weaknesses, the evidence or argument on which it is based. You consider its 'valu' to your situation or problem, where it might be useful, what its limitations are.

EVALUATE

Apply

Transfer the understanding you have gained from your critical evaluation and use in response to questions, assignments and projects.	**Apply**	

We are now getting towards the top of the staircase. The great buzz with learning comes when you find that ideas can transform the way you see or do things. On the surface perhaps nothing has changed, but you know you see things differently. You understand. You have become someone who can use – or reject or refute – ideas or approaches in your own work, whether this is a further exploration of ideas, or whether there is a more direct application for your insights as a practitioner.

Adapted from Godwin (2009)

Justify

Use critical thinking to develop arguments, draw conclusions, make inferences and identify implications.	**Justify**

This is where you stand up and are counted. You are able to say not only what you did or thought but *why* you did it or thought it. You are able to argue, defend, justify. Your essay will have the **golden thread of argument**, running from start to finish, from introduction to conclusion. Better still, you may end with the 'What if? What next?' questions – the implications.

So what is that critical thing? I hope you can now see that the critical dimension is a mindset you bring to your work. You can do it once you have the confidence to take control of your studies. It is a bit like turning a little chunk of rock in the sun and suddenly seeing the light catch a sparkle.

There is nothing magical about it, but you do have to work at it. At no point does good work just happen. It is the outcome of reading, analysis, reflection, asking questions, and then recording the outcomes of this process in *your* writing. It is hard work.

Writing is a craft: if you work at it, you will get better at it. When you start to rewrite your work because you want it to be better, you know you are a writer – and a critical one at that. When you are a writer, your 'voice' will come through: it is your analysis, reflection and interpretation in *your* words. Let's hope your reader in turn will feel moved to write:

> *'You have engaged with the debates in the subject and your critical analysis is of a high standard …'*

Go for it!

References

Belbin M (1993). *Team roles at work*. Oxford: Elsevier Butterworth Heinemann.

Boddy D (2008). *Management: an introduction*, 4th edition. Harlow: Pearson.

Godfrey J (2009). *Reading and making notes.* Basingstoke: Palgrave Macmillan.

Godfrey J (2011). *Writing for university.* Basingstoke: Palgrave Macmillan.

Godwin J (2009). *Planning your essay.* Basingstoke: Palgrave Macmillan.

Guirdham M (2002). *Interactive behaviour at work*, 3rd edition. Harlow: Pearson.

Open University (2013). *Critical thinking.* © 2013 The Open University.

Osborne T and Kiker C (2005). Carbon offsets as an economic alternative to large-scale logging: a case study in Guyama. *Ecological Economics* 52(4) (1 March), 481–96. Elsevier ScienceDirect.

RMIT (2013). *Essay planning: read and take notes.* Available at http://emedia.rmit.edu.au/learninglab/content/read-and-take-notes [Accessed 25 October 2013]

Shorter Oxford English Dictionary (1983). 3rd edition. Oxford: Oxford University Press.

Tuckman BW and Jensen MA (1977). Stages in small group development revisited. *Group and Organisation Studies* 2, 419–27.

University of Cambridge (no date). *Research skills programme: How to read 10 books in an hour.* Available at: www.reading.ac.uk/web/FILES/sta/10_books_an_hour.pdf [Accessed 25 October 2013].

Williams K (1995). *Writing essays.* Developing writing series. Oxford: Oxford Centre for Staff Development.

Williams K (1996). *Essential writing skills.* Developing writing series. Oxford: Oxford Centre for Staff Development.

Williams K (2013). *Planning your dissertation.* Basingstoke: Palgrave Macmillan.

Williams K and Reid M (2011). *Time management.* Basingstoke: Palgrave Macmillan.

Williams K, Woolliams M and Spiro J (2012). *Reflective writing.* Basingstoke: Palgrave Macmillan.

Useful sources

Aveyard H, Sharp P and Woolliams M (2011). *A beginner's guide to critical thinking in health and social care.* Maidenhead: Open University Press.

Critical thinking has particular importance in health and social care in evaluating research evidence. This book offers detailed guidance and considers the importance of critical thinking in professional life.

Cottrell S (2011). *Critical thinking skills*, 2nd edition. Basingstoke: Palgrave Macmillan.

A thorough but accessible guide to developing critical thinking skills in your studies, with examples and activities: from exploring your approach, through reading, argument and in different writing tasks.

RMIT (2013). *Learning lab*. Available at http://emedia.rmit.edu.au/learninglab/.

From the home page, choose your area: writing skills, assessment tasks, postgraduate and more. In a few clicks you will find superb advice, clearly set out, with uncluttered, visual pages, and next to no scrolling.

University of Manchester (2005). *Academic phrasebank*. Available at www.phrasebank.manchester.ac.uk/index.htm

Designed for academic writers in general, it is a superb resource for anyone looking for words and phrases to use in their writing. It is user friendly, well organised – a must!

Index